I JUST WANT TO BE A BUSINESSWOMAN

An inspirational journey that encourages entrepreneurship for children

TIANA VON JOHNSON

PUBLISHED BY: Tiana Von Johnson Worldwide, LLC.

30 Wall St, 8th Fl, NY, NY 10005

DISCLAIMER AND/OR LEGAL NOTICES

While all attempts have been made to verify information provided in this book and its ancillary materials, neither the author nor publisher assumes responsibility for errors, inaccuracies, or omissions and is not responsible for any monetary loss in any matter. If advice concerning legal, financial, accounting or related matters is needed, the services of a qualified professional should be sought. This book or is associated ancillary materials, including verbal and written training, is not intended for use as a source of legal, financial, or accounting advice. You should be aware of the various laws governing business transactions or other business practices in your state. The information contained in this book is strictly for educational purpose. Therefore, if you wish to apply ideas contained in this book, you are taking full responsibility for your actions. There is no guarantee or promise, expressed or implied, that you will earn any money using the strategies, concepts, techniques, exercises and ideas in the book.

STANDARD EARNINGS AND INCOME DISCLAIMER

With respect to the reliability, accuracy, timeliness, usefulness, adequacy, completeness, and/or suitability of information provided in this book, Tiana Von Johnson Worldwide, LLC. its partners' associates, affiliates, consultants, and/or presenters make no warranties, guarantees, representations, or claims of any kind. Participants' results will vary depending on many factors. All claims or representations as to income earning are not considered as average earnings. All products and services are for educational and informational purposes only. Check with your accountant, attorney, or professional advisor before acting on this or any information. By continuing with reading this book, you agree that Tiana Von Johnson Worldwide, LLC. is not responsible for the success or failure of your personal, business, or financial decisions relating to any information.

PRINTED IN THE UNITED STATES OF AMERICA | FIRST EDITION

This book is for the young girl who is where I was at seven-years-old. That girl from the Bronx who had big dreams. The girl who saw life differently and had so much greatness in her. The girl that had a burning desire to always push forward and do big things. The girl who was willing to stop at nothing to bring her vision of entrepreneurship to life. Stay focused!

-Tiana Von Johnson

TO:

_____

FROM:

_____

DATE:

_____

It was a bright Friday afternoon at P.S. 87 Elementary School in the Bronx, New York. The bell rang, students were rushing to different classrooms, locker doors slammed and there was a great deal chatter.

4

Mrs. Jacob, the teacher whom the kids loved so much, was busy discussing different jobs for career day.

"Students, can anyone tell me what a doctor does?" she asked.

"A doctor is someone who takes care of sick people" the students answered.

"How about an engineer?" she continued.

"An engineer is someone who builds cars" replied the students.

"Correct. An engineer not only builds cars but also makes houses, airplanes, ships, roads and many other things."

8

Reynah, a student who was confused, replied "Mrs. Jacob, but my dad is an engineer, he doesn't build any of these things. My dad works in the refinery."

"That's right, an engineer can also work in the refinery and so many other places" Mrs. Jacob replied. "Now tell me, Reynah, what do you want to be when you grow up?"

Now, tell me, class, "What do you want to be when you grow up?"

"I want to be a doctor"
shouted Ryan from the
back of the class.

13

"I want to be a lawyer" exclaimed Alana.

"What does a lawyer do?" asked Mrs. Jacob.

Aa Bb Cc Dd

"A lawyer helps people not to go to jail" replied Alana.

"Well, yes that is partially right. A lawyer represents innocent and not so innocent people in the court.

Tatiana became disappointed as she heard more answers from her classmates. She didn't want to become a doctor, lawyer or engineer. She wanted to become something very different.

17

"Anyone else?" The teacher continued.

"I want to be a firefighter," said Devin from the middle of the class.

"That's good," replied Mrs. Jacob.

"Hi there Tatiana,
you look sad.
Are you okay?"

"I am fine,"
Tatiana
replied.

19

"Now tell us. What do you want to be, Tatiana?"

She looked up at the teacher, "I don't know."

The class became quiet as every eye turned on Tatiana.

"Surely you know. Tell us," urged Mrs. Jacob.

20

"I don't know," she replied while fiddling her fingers. She was nervous about what everyone would think.

"You must have an idea of what you want to be," Mrs. Jacob replied.

"I... I want to be a businesswoman" Tatiana replied timidly.

22

"A businesswoman?"
asked Mrs. Jacob
surprised.

"Yes, ma'am," Tatiana replied.

24

"I want to be Batman when I grow up," shouted Tristen, the class clown from the back of the class.

The silence was lifted, and the whole class burst into laughter.

Tatiana grew more frustrated as the class was laughing and slowly she couldn't hear the class laughing anymore...

26

Tatiana went into a daydream about her life as a businesswoman...

Tatiana is finishing her business meeting in the boardroom.

"I will be traveling over the next few days. Please stay focused on the mission and I will see you all next week when I return."

Hurrying along the corridor of her office, Tatiana is headed to the parking garage as her secretary walks with her.

"Nicole, don't forget to call Mr. McKenzie. He needs to be reminded that I'll be stopping by at his office in Paris on my way back from Italy." Tatiana instructed.

"Yes, ma'am," I spoke with him this morning. He will be waiting for you."

"Great. Has my new product order been delivered to the warehouse yet?" Tatiana asked.

"Not yet. They called in to send their apologies. They are delayed due to technical issues," replied Nicole.

"By the way, call Mr. Lewis, the administrator at the business school. Inform him I will not make it to this week's guest lecture but thank him for the invitation and let him know that I can come next week if they will have me.

"Okay, ma'am. I will do just that," Nicole replied.

They went down to the underground garage where Tatiana's driver was waiting to take them to the airport.

Tatiana was headed to Italy to provide the keynote speech at the World Business Summit, a gathering of the world's top businesspeople.

As they entered the garage, the driver was standing beside the car, Tatiana felt someone touch her on the back, she turned back and woke up from her daydream as Tristen tapped her shoulder...

"Batman, really?"
Mrs. Jacobs grew
frustrated with
Tristen joking in the
class.

I'm sorry Mrs. Jacobs.

I'm sorry Tatiana, I was just playing around, Tristen said.

"Tatiana, I think that
is really amazing,"
Mrs. Jacob said.

Tatiana was excited. She couldn't wait to pursue her dreams and become a businesswoman.

The classroom bell rang, and the students started to get out of their seats—except Tatiana.

"That is the end of today's class. Have a nice weekend."

"Thank you, ma'am. Have a nice weekend too," chorused the students who were happy they did not have school the next day.

As the students left, Mrs. Jacob walked towards Tatiana's desk. Tatiana was nervous because she didn't know what to expect.

"Always choose what you want to become according to what you love. Find your passion and never be afraid to live out your dreams... even your daydreams," Mrs. Jacob said to Tatiana with a smile.

"Thank you, Mrs. Jacobs. I just want to be a businesswoman"

For the next few years, Tatiana worked on her passions of becoming just that--a businesswoman!

I JUST WANT TO BE A BUSINESSWOMAN

I JUST WANT TO BE A BUSINESSWOMAN

_____

_____

_____

_____

_____

_____

_____

_____

_____

_____

_____

I JUST WANT TO BE A BUSINESSWOMAN

_____

_____

_____

_____

_____

_____

_____

_____

_____

_____

_____

I JUST WANT TO BE A BUSINESSWOMAN

_____

_____

_____

_____

_____

_____

_____

_____

_____

_____

_____

_____

I JUST WANT TO BE A BUSINESSWOMAN

_____

_____

_____

_____

_____

_____

_____

_____

_____

_____

_____

I JUST WANT TO BE A BUSINESSWOMAN

_____

_____

_____

_____

_____

_____

_____

_____

_____

_____

_____

I JUST WANT TO BE A BUSINESSWOMAN

_____

_____

_____

_____

_____

_____

_____

_____

_____

_____

_____

63390604R00031